Let's LEARN the BIBLE for Early Readers

Trisha White Priebe

Let's LEARN the BIBLE for Early Readers

A Kid's Guide to God's Word

BARBOUR kidz
A Division of Barbour Publishing

ISBN 979-8-89151-287-0

Published by Barbour Publishing, Inc., 1810 Barbour Drive, Uhrichsville, Ohio 44683, www.barbourbooks.com

Our mission is to inspire the world with the life-changing message of the Bible.

Printed in China.
002811 0126 XY

For the kids at Central,
this book is for you—with the hope
that you will learn to love God's Word
with your whole heart for your whole
life. There is truly nothing better.
You are loved and prayed for every day.

TABLE OF CONTENTS

Section Four

Section Five

Section Six

LET'S LEARN THE BIBLE!

You have made a very good choice. This choice could change your life!

By reading this book, you will **learn more about God.** You will start to understand His Word. And you will discover His very good plan for your life. This book explains **the most important Book in the world.** That's the Bible!

The Bible isn't just old stories. It's not a book for rainy days, when you can't go outside. No! The Bible is alive! It helps you to know truth. It gives you hope. It is a comfort when you feel sad. The Bible is like a telescope you can use to see God. It's like a mirror you use to see yourself. The Bible is really **the Word of God.**

Does the Bible seem too big? Is it hard to understand? That's okay—lots of people feel that way. But this book will help. You will meet great Bible heroes. You will find exciting promises from God. And you will learn truth to help you every day.

Are you ready to explore the best Book ever? ***Let's learn the Bible!***

Section One

WHAT IS THE BIBLE?

WHAT MAKES THE BIBLE SO SPECIAL?

The Bible is the Word of God. That means God talks to you through the Bible. It is not like any other book. That's because *God* made it. He told people to write down what He wanted you to know. God "breathed out" what He wanted the Bible writers to say. Then those writers put God's thoughts into their own words.

The Bible is a big book! But it is more than that. **The Bible is like a library.** It is made up of **66 smaller books**. They were written by many different men. And they were written over a long time. . .more than a thousand years. **The Bible tells us who God is.** It tells us how much He loves us. It tells us how we can know Him. The Bible is full of truth we need to live good, happy lives.

God's Word gives us strength and hope.
ROMANS 15:4

Have you ever used a flashlight in the dark? **The Bible is like a flashlight.** It shows us what is right. It helps us to make good choices. When we read and follow God's Word, good things happen. The Bible lights our way and helps us stay on the right path.

Your Word is a lamp to my feet
and a light to my path.
PSALM 119:105

For the word is a lamp.
The teaching is a light,
and strong words that punish
are the way of life.
PROVERBS 6:23

HOW CAN THE BIBLE HELP ME?

The Bible is full of wisdom. That means it teaches us good things. The Bible tells us how we should live. **God's Word helps us understand what's right.** It shows us how to please God. The Bible is much better than any other book!

The Bible can help you grow closer to God. When you read the Bible, you find out who God really is. You learn about His love and power. You find out what He's like and how much He cares for you.

The Bible can help you make wise choices. The Bible is full of stories that show you how to make good decisions. Wise choices honor God. Wise choices give you a better life.

The Bible can help with your feelings. The Bible talks about emotions. Emotions are feelings. Sometimes we get angry or sad or worried. The Bible helps us to honor God even when we're upset.

God made people to have emotions. The Bible shows us that God cares about our feelings. We can take all of our feelings to Him. We can trust Him to help us through hard times. God wants to give us His peace.

But You, O Lord, are a God full of love and pity.
You are slow to anger and rich in
loving-kindness and truth.
PSALM 86:15

Big Idea

No matter what you're feeling today, there's a Bible verse to help!

GOD'S WORD FOR BIG FEELINGS

When You're Mad

A gentle answer turns away anger,
but a sharp word causes anger.
PROVERBS 15:1

When You're Sad

The Lord is near to those who have a broken heart.
And He saves those who are broken in spirit.
PSALM 34:18

When You're Scared

"Do not fear, for I am with you.
Do not be afraid, for I am your God.
I will give you strength."
ISAIAH 41:10

When You're Happy

It is good to give thanks to the Lord,
and sing praises to Your name, O Most High.
PSALM 92:1

WHY SHOULD I READ THE BIBLE?

You are just learning to read. That is a great thing!

The Bible can be hard to read. But you have your whole life to learn it. You are smart to start reading the Bible now.

Remember this: **The Bible is God's Word to us.** It is filled with God's love and wisdom. The Bible will change your life.

Reading the Bible can be fun. It's not something we *have* to do. It's something we *get* to do. **We read the Bible so we can know God better.** And we read the Bible to know how to please God.

Rhyme It!

Always do the things you should.
God is pleased when you do good.

Want to know God better? Here are some verses to help you:

"You will look for Me and find Me,
when you look for Me with all your heart."
JEREMIAH 29:13

Look for the Lord while He may be found.
Call upon Him while He is near.
ISAIAH 55:6

God has shown His love to us by
sending His only Son into the world.
God did this so we might have
life through Christ. This is love!
It is not that we loved God
but that He loved us.
1 JOHN 4:9–10

Want to learn how to please God? Here are some verses to help:

*Oh man, He has told you what is good.
What does the Lord ask of you but
to do what is fair and to love kindness,
and to walk without pride with your God?*
MICAH 6:8

*You must be kind to each other.
Think of the other person. Forgive other
people just as God forgave you because
of Christ's death on the cross.*
EPHESIANS 4:32

HOW DOES GOD SPEAK TO ME?

Did you ever get a letter in the mail? It's fun! A message that is just for you is special. It makes you feel important and loved.

The Bible is like a letter from God. It is His message written just for you!

Some people wonder how God talks. We don't hear His voice. But He "talks" through His Word, the Bible. It is full of God's truth. It is full of His wisdom. It is full of His love. When you read the Bible, you hear from God Himself.

Think of the Bible as God's note just to you. He asks you to know Him better and follow His ways. The Bible is not just any book! It is a letter from the God who made you. It is a letter from the God who wants to be with you.

What could be better than that?

Rhyme It!

**God is love! He'll even sing
when you take Him as your King.**

God has a lot to say to you in His Word. Here are a few important verses. Try to find each one in your own Bible. Try to read God's own words to you:

God has a good plan for your life.
Read Jeremiah 29:11

God will always be with you,
no matter where you go.
Read Matthew 28:20

God is working things out for your good,
even when things seem bad.
Read Romans 8:28

God cares about what you feel—so don't be
afraid to share your feelings with Him.
Read 1 Peter 5:7

Wow! The God who made the whole world wants to talk to *you*. He made the earth. He made the oceans. He made every living thing. But He thinks *you* are very important.

ACTIVITY:

How Well Do You Know God's Word?

Let's see if you can remember what you just read. Each question has three possible answers. Choose the answer you think is right. It's okay if you don't know all the answers. This is a great way to learn more!

1. What is the Bible?

    a) a collection of poems

    b) a special letter from God to you

    c) a book of science facts

2. What does the Bible say it is like?

    a) a light

    b) a radio

    c) a fancy house

3. What is one way the Bible can help you?

    a) it helps you understand how to cook

    b) it shows you how to make money

    c) it helps you grow closer to God

4. When you're feeling angry, what does the Bible say?

    a) a gentle answer turns away anger

    b) shout at everyone

    c) ignore your feelings

5. What does the Bible say about God's plan for your life?

    a) it's a secret, so don't try to figure it out

    b) you have to make your own plan

    c) God has a good plan for your life

Okay, the quiz is done. Turn the page to check your answers. Let's see how much you've learned!

Scoring

4–5 correct: You're a Bible smarty! Keep reading and learning to know God better every day.

3 correct: Great job! You're on your way to knowing God's Word even better.

1–2 correct: Nice work! There's more to discover. . .keep reading your Bible.

0 correct: It's okay! God's Word is full of treasure—keep reading and you'll learn more.

Section Two

WHERE DID THE BIBLE COME FROM?

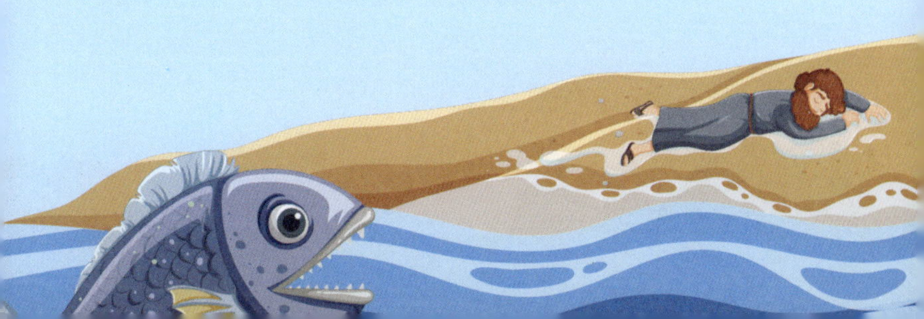

HOW GOD GAVE US HIS WORD

The Bible was written over many years. It was written by lots of people. They lived in different places. They had all kinds of jobs. Some were shepherds. Others were kings. Some were fishermen. One was a doctor! But they were all alike in one way. **God gave the Bible authors a message to write.**

All the Holy Writings are God-given
and are made alive by Him.
2 TIMOTHY 3:16

No part of the Holy Writings came long ago
because of what man wanted to write.
But holy men who belonged to God
spoke what the Holy Spirit told them.
2 PETER 1:21

The Bible tells us that **it was "breathed out" by God.** He gave every writer His ideas. Then God made sure they wrote just what He wanted us to know. The writers used their own words. But God guided them the whole time.

The Bible took a long time to write. It took more than one thousand years! But every part of the Bible fits together. God was in charge. He made sure **His message is clear and correct.**

We can know that God gave us the words in the Bible. It often tells us, "This is what the Lord says." You can be sure the words that follow come straight from God.

God's Word is living and powerful.
It is sharper than a sword that cuts both ways.
It cuts straight into where the soul and spirit meet
and it divides them. It cuts into the joints and bones.
It tells what the heart is thinking about
and what it wants to do.
HEBREWS 4:12

Here are some of the words God spoke:

This is what the Lord Who made the heavens, the God Who planned and made the earth, and everything in it and did not make it a waste place, but made it a place for people to live in, says, "I am the Lord, and there is no other."
ISAIAH 45:18

The Lord says, "Cursed is the man who trusts in man, who trusts in the flesh for his strength, and whose heart turns away from the Lord."
JEREMIAH 17:5

" 'For I know the plans I have for you,' says the Lord, 'plans for well-being and not for trouble, to give you a future and a hope.' "
JEREMIAH 29:11

God speaks to His people to teach them. He speaks to His people to give them courage. Can you find other verses like these in your Bible?

WHO WROTE THE BIBLE?

God used more than forty different writers. That means God had a whole team of people. He wanted to share His really good story with you. Why did God do that? So you could know Him better! God wants you to learn to live for Him.

Now, let's get to know some of those Bible authors. Let's see how God used them to write His Word!

Moses

Moses is a famous Bible author. He wrote the first five books of the Bible. Moses told about creation. He wrote about God's laws. Moses is famous for leading God's people out of Egypt. They had been slaves there! God spoke to Moses in special ways. Moses wrote down what God told him.

The Lord spoke to Moses face to face,
as a man speaks to his friend.
EXODUS 33:11

David

David was a king. He was also a brave soldier. He was even a song writer! David wrote many of the Psalms. Psalms are songs and prayers to God. David's heart was full of love for God. He poured out his feelings through his songs. Some of David's psalms are still sung in churches today.

David the son of Jesse,
the man who was raised on high,
the chosen one of the God of Jacob,
the sweet song writer of Israel. . .
2 SAMUEL 23:1

Isaiah

Isaiah wrote the book called by his name. He spoke to kings. He spoke to regular people. He said they needed to do right. Isaiah wrote "prophecies." Those are truthful messages about the future. Isaiah told about God's plan to send a Savior. That was Jesus!

At that time the Lord spoke through
Isaiah the son of Amoz, saying. . .
ISAIAH 20:2

Paul

Paul was a Christian leader who wrote many letters. Some of his letters are now books in the New Testament. Paul told how to live for God. He told how to love other people. And Paul told how Jesus changed everything for the better.

You can be sure the long waiting of our Lord is part of His plan to save men from the punishment of sin. God gave our dear brother Paul the wisdom to write about this also.
2 PETER 3:15

John

John was one of Jesus' special followers. He wrote the Gospel of John. He also wrote four other books. John tells us how much God loves us. John tells us we should love each other. John also told what would happen when Jesus comes again!

John tells that the Word of God is true. He tells of Jesus Christ and all that he saw and heard of Him. The man who reads this Book and listens to it being read and obeys what it says will be happy.
REVELATION 1:2–3

HOW DID THE BIBLE COME TOGETHER?

The Bible took more than one thousand years to write. It was written by about forty different men. God used so many people to give us His Word. He took so much time. It must be very important!

Let's see how the Bible was written.

The Books of Moses

(written about 1,400 years before Jesus was born)

Moses wrote the first five books of the Bible. He told where the world came from. He told about the first people. And Moses told about God's rules.

Moses wrote the words of this Law in a book from beginning to the end.
DEUTERONOMY 31:24

The Prophets

(written before Jesus was born)

People called *prophets* taught God's plan. They told how people should live for God.

Mercies and forgivenesses belong to the Lord our God, though we have rebelled against Him. Nor have we obeyed the voice of the LORD our God to walk in His laws, which He set before us by His servants the prophets.
DANIEL 9:9–10 SKJV

The Gospels

(written after Jesus lived)

Matthew, Mark, Luke, and John wrote about Jesus' life. Their books are called "Gospels." That means "good news"! The Gospels tell about Jesus' teaching. They tell about His miracles. They also tell how Jesus died and came back to life.

Many people have written about the things that have happened among us. Those who saw everything from the first and helped teach the Good News have passed these things on to us. Dear Theophilus, I have looked with care into these things from the beginning. I have decided it would be good to write them to you.

LUKE 1:1–3

Letters to the Early Church

(written after Jesus lived)

Wise men like Paul wrote letters to the early Christians. These letters tell us how to live for God. They tell us how to love others.

When this letter has been read to you, have it read in the church in Laodicea also. Be sure you read the letter that is coming from Laodicea.

COLOSSIANS 4:16

Revelation

(written after Jesus lived)

John wrote the last book of the Bible. It is called *Revelation*. This book tells what will happen when Jesus comes to earth a second time.

> *The things that are written in the Book are made known by Jesus Christ. God gave these things to Christ so He could show them to the servants He owns. These are things which must happen very soon. Christ sent His angel to John who is a servant owned by Him. Christ made these things known to John.*
>
> REVELATION 1:1

Over hundreds of years, God "inspired" people to write His message. That means He "breathed out" the words and ideas. Then the Bible authors wrote God's thoughts in their own words. Many of these writers were people like you and me. God used them to share His love and His plans for the world.

The best part? **You get to read God's Word today!** Every bit of the Bible will help you to know God better.

> *I will be glad in Your Law, which I love.*
> *I will lift up my hands to Your Word,*
> *which I love, and I will think about Your Law.*
>
> PSALM 119:47–48

HOW WAS THE BIBLE MADE?

In the beginning, the Bible wasn't a book like you hold right now. **The Bible was first written on scrolls.** Scrolls are long sheets of stuff for writing. They are made from animal skins or a plant called papyrus. These scrolls were rolled up and kept safe.

The Bible was first written by hand. There were no printers or copy machines to help. People called "scribes" did the work. They had been taught to write things down. They double-checked their work all the time. They wanted to be sure the message stayed the same.

Scribes spent many hours watching for mistakes. One wrong letter could change the meaning of God's Word. They didn't want that! **The Bible is too important to be careless.**

Try Being a Scribe

Try copying God's Word like a scribe. See how well you can do!

Pick one of these verses to copy. Write it on a piece of paper or in a notebook. Copy it as perfectly as you can, just like the scribes did.

Your Word is a lamp to my feet
and a light to my path.
PSALM 119:105

The Lord your God is with you, a Powerful
One Who wins the battle. He will have much joy
over you. With His love He will give you new life.
He will have joy over you with loud singing.
ZEPHANIAH 3:17

"For God so loved the world that He gave His only Son. Whoever puts his trust in God's Son will not be lost but will have life that lasts forever."
JOHN 3:16

I can do all things because Christ gives me the strength.
PHILIPPIANS 4:13

We love Him because He loved us first.
1 JOHN 4:19

Now share your copied verse with someone! Show it to a friend. Show it to your mom or dad. Show it to your pastor. Tell them why you picked that verse and what it means to you.

THINGS TO KNOW ABOUT THE BIBLE

By now you know the Bible is a special book. The Bible's story is full of surprises.

Here are ten things to know about the Bible. **It is the most important book ever written!**

The grass dries up.
The flower loses its color.
But the Word of our God stands forever.
ISAIAH 40:8

#1: It Used to Take a Long Time to Make One Bible

Big machines print Bibles today. But before machines, every Bible had to be copied by hand. It could take months to finish a single Bible. Or it might even take years.

#2: The Bible Has Been Protected Through History

Many people have tried to destroy the Bible. But God never let them win. God keeps His Word safe so that we can read it today.

"Heaven and earth will pass away, but My words will not pass away."
MATTHEW 24:35

#3: The Bible Is the Best-Selling Book Ever

The Bible is the world's most important Book. And there are more Bibles in the world than any other book.

#4: The Bible Was Written for Everyone

The Bible was written for all people. It doesn't matter where they live. It doesn't matter how old they are. It doesn't matter what language they speak. That means the Bible was written for *you*.

This is what the LORD says: "Heaven is My throne, and the earth is My footstool. . . . My hand has made all those things, and all those things have been," says the LORD. "But I will look to this man, even to him who is poor and of a contrite spirit and who trembles at My word."

ISAIAH 66:1–2 SKJV

#5: Bible Chapters and Verses Came Later

When the Bible was first written, there were no chapters and verses. They were added about a thousand years ago. They make it easier to find parts of God's Word.

#6: The Bible Talks About Many People and Events

The Bible talks about kings in Egypt. It talks about rulers in Rome. It talks about things that happened long ago. And they are all true!

#7: The Bible Was Written in Different Places

Have you heard of Asia? Have you heard of Africa? Have you heard of Europe? These are all places where the Bible was written.

#8: The Bible Is Found in Many Languages

The Bible was written in three languages. Today you can find the whole Bible in more than 750! Parts of the Bible can be read in more than a thousand languages.

"Your blood has bought men for God from every family and from every language and from every kind of people and from every nation."
REVELATION 5:9

#9: The Bible Has Been Snuck into Secret Places

Some rulers try to keep the Bible out of their countries. But people who love God's Word sneak it in. They could be killed if they are caught. But they keep trying. They want people to know and love the Bible like they do.

#10: YOU Can Keep God's Word Going!

You can read the Bible. You can memorize the Bible. You can share the Bible. When you do, you're part of the Bible's story. You are helping to keep God's Word alive in people's hearts.

He said to me, "Son of man, take all My words that I say to you into your heart, and hear with your ears. Then go to the Jews who have been taken away from their land. Go to the sons of your people. And if they listen or not, tell them, 'This is what the Lord God says.'"

EZEKIEL 3:10–11

Section Three

WHAT'S IN THE BIBLE?

THE BIBLE: GOD'S LIBRARY OF BOOKS

The Bible is more than a book. **The Bible is like a library.** The word *Bible* comes from another word that means "books."

Here is what you'll find in this library:

Testaments

The Bible has two main parts. They are called *testaments*. The Old Testament and the New Testament are the two big parts of God's story.

Books

There are 66 books in the Old and New Testaments. Some books are mainly stories. Some books are full of songs. Some books share wise sayings. Some books are personal letters. Each book has its own name. Here are the Bible's books, in order:

Genesis
Exodus
Leviticus
Numbers
Deuteronomy

Joshua
Judges
Ruth
1–2 Samuel
1–2 Kings

1–2 Chronicles
Ezra
Nehemiah
Esther
Job

Psalms
Proverbs
Ecclesiastes
Song of Solomon
Isaiah
Jeremiah
Lamentations
Ezekiel
Daniel
Hosea
Joel
Amos
Obadiah
Jonah
Micah
Nahum
Habakkuk
Zephaniah
Haggai
Zechariah
Malachi
Matthew
Mark
Luke
John
Acts
Romans
1–2 Corinthians
Galatians
Ephesians
Philippians
Colossians
1–2 Thessalonians
1–2 Timothy
Titus
Philemon
Hebrews
James
1–2 Peter
1–3 John
Jude
Revelation

Chapters

Each Bible book is made up of *chapters*. Chapters are the biggest parts of each book. Look at your Bible. You will see big numbers on nearly every page. Those numbers tell you the chapter you're reading. If you open up to the book of Genesis and see a big 1, you're in Genesis chapter 1.

Verses

Each chapter is made up of *verses*. Here is a famous Bible verse: "For God so loved the world that He gave His only Son. Whoever puts his trust in God's Son will not be lost but will have life that lasts forever." That is "John 3:16." It is in the book of John, chapter 3, verse 16.

References

You can put the book name, the chapter, and verse numbers together. Then you have a *reference*. John 3:16; Genesis 1:1; and Revelation 22:20 are all references.

This book tells you about the Bible. But don't just read *about* the Bible. ***Read your Bible!*** Explore it. Visit the library of God's books. It is full of important truths for you to learn.

The Laws of the Lord are right,
giving joy to the heart.
The Word of the Lord is pure,
giving light to the eyes.
PSALM 19:8

DIFFERENT KINDS OF WRITING

Here's a fancy word: *genre*. Say it like this: JOHN-ruh. *Genre* just means a kind of writing.

Think about movies you've watched. Some movies are funny. Some movies are a little scary. Some movies are exciting. God's Word is like that. There are different kinds of writing in the Bible. **Each kind of writing tells God's story in a special way.**

Let's look at some of the types of writing in the Bible!

History (Old Testament)

This kind of writing tells true stories. History is about people and what they did a long time ago. You'll find stories about kings and battles. You'll see how God rescued His people.

The Books: Genesis, Exodus, Leviticus, Numbers, Deuteronomy, Joshua, Judges, Ruth, 1–2 Samuel, 1–2 Kings, 1–2 Chronicles, Ezra, Nehemiah, Esther

Poems

Bible poems are pretty. But these poems do not rhyme. Bible poems help us to know God's love. Bible poems help us to share our feelings with Him.

The Book: Psalms

Wisdom

Wisdom books are about pleasing God. They are full of important lessons. They tell about life. They teach good choices. They help us to know what's important.

The Books: Job, Proverbs, Ecclesiastes, Song of Solomon

Prophecy (Old Testament)

Say it like this: PRAH-fuh-see. God gave His words to special men called prophets. They told people what God planned to do. They shared His good promises with others.

The Books: Isaiah, Jeremiah, Lamentations, Ezekiel, Daniel, Hosea, Joel, Amos, Obadiah, Jonah, Micah, Nahum, Habakkuk, Zephaniah, Haggai, Zechariah, Malachi

Gospels

The Gospels are books that tell the story of Jesus. In the Gospels, you see Jesus' birth. You read about His miracles. You learn His teaching. You see His death on the cross. And you see Him come back to life! *Gospel* means "good news."

The Books: Matthew, Mark, Luke, John

History (New Testament)

This kind of writing tells how Jesus' church began. When Jesus went back to heaven, He sent His Holy Spirit to earth. The Spirit helped Jesus' followers share His good news. The church grew and grew!

The Book: Acts

Epistles

Epistle is a fancy word that means "letter." These letters were written by leaders like Paul and Peter. They wanted to help people follow Jesus.

The Books: Romans, 1–2 Corinthians, Galatians, Ephesians, Philippians, Colossians, 1–2 Thessalonians, 1–2 Timothy, Titus, Philemon, Hebrews, James, 1–2 Peter, 1–3 John, Jude

Prophecy (New Testament)

There's only one book of this kind in the New Testament. It tells about the end of time. It shows God's plan for making the world new.

The Book: Revelation

What Is Your Favorite?

Each kind of Bible writing is special. Each kind shows a different part of who God is or how He wants us to live. There are stories about brave heroes. There are poems about God's goodness. There is teaching about how to live right. Every word in the Bible helps to tell the greatest story ever told. God's story!

Think About It!

Which kind of Bible writing is most interesting to you? Why?

WHAT IS THE OLD TESTAMENT?

The Old Testament is the first big part of the Bible. It is made up of 39 books. Genesis is the first book. Malachi is the last. **The Old Testament helps us know who God is.** It shows how all things point to Jesus. Here are some of the big ideas of the Old Testament:

God's Creation

The Old Testament starts at the very beginning. We learn that God made all things. He made our earth. He made the sun and stars. He made animals and plants. And then He made people! God made things very good. He wanted us to live in a happy, healthy world. But people soon messed things up. They "sinned" when they disobeyed God.

In the beginning God made from nothing
the heavens and the earth.
GENESIS 1:1

And God made man in His own likeness. In the likeness
of God He made him. He made both male and female.
And God wanted good to come to them,
saying, "Give birth to many. Grow in number.
Fill the earth and rule over it."
GENESIS 1:27–28

The History of Israel

God loved a special people called "Israel." He chose them to show the world how good He is. God chose Abraham first. Men like Moses and King David were part of Israel. God always cared for His people. But they didn't always follow Him.

God called to him from inside the bush, saying, "Moses, Moses!" Moses answered, "Here I am." God said, "Do not come near. Take your shoes off your feet. For the place where you are standing is holy ground." He said also, "I am the God of your father, the God of Abraham, the God of Isaac, and the God of Jacob. . . . I have seen the suffering of My people in Egypt. I have heard their cry because of the men who make them work. I know how they suffer. So I have come down to save them from the power of the Egyptians. I will bring them out of that land to a good big land, to a land flowing with milk and honey."

EXODUS 3:4–8

The Law

God gave His people rules. He called His rules "the law." The law helped Israel know how to live. These rules were about loving God and other people. The Ten Commandments were part of the law.

"And you must love the Lord your God with all your heart and with all your soul and with all your strength."

DEUTERONOMY 6:5

Prophecies of Jesus

Do you know the best thing about the Old Testament? It points to Jesus! God said He would send a Savior. Jesus would save God's people from sin. Prophets wrote about this long before Jesus was born.

The Old Testament gets us ready for the New Testament. God wrote the whole story. That's why everything fits together just right.

"Bethlehem Ephrathah, you are too little to be among the family groups of Judah. But from you One will come who will rule for Me in Israel. His coming was planned long ago, from the beginning."
MICAH 5:2

WHAT IS THE NEW TESTAMENT?

The New Testament is the last part of the Bible. It tells the story of Jesus.

Jesus is God! He is one person of the "Trinity"—God the Father, God the Son, and God the Holy Spirit. God made the world. Then people messed it up with sin. So Jesus came to earth as a man. He died on a cross to pay the price for people's sin. We are saved when we believe in Him.

The New Testament is the last 27 books of the Bible. They tell about God's love through Jesus. They help us to know God's plan for the whole world.

Jesus came and said to them, "All power has been given to Me in heaven and on earth. Go and make followers of all the nations. Baptize them in the name of the Father and of the Son and of the Holy Spirit. Teach them to do all the things I have told you."

MATTHEW 28:18–20

Here are some big ideas in the New Testament:

The Life of Jesus

The New Testament starts with four books called *Gospels*. Matthew, Mark, Luke, and John tell us about Jesus. We see His birth. We learn of His miracles. We read His teaching. We find out about His love for people. The Gospels also tell how Jesus died on the cross, then came back to life to save us. That is very good news. The word *Gospel* means "good news"!

Jesus went on to all the towns and cities. He taught in their places of worship. He preached the Good News of the holy nation of God. He healed every sickness and disease the people had.
MATTHEW 9:35

The Early Church

Jesus went back to heaven. But just before He left, He gave His followers a job. They should share the good news of Jesus with all people. The book of Acts tells how the first churches started. Acts shows that people began to follow Jesus all over the world.

Then those who gladly received his word were baptized, and the same day about three thousand souls were added to them. And they continued steadfastly in the apostles' doctrine and fellowship and in the breaking of bread and in prayers.
ACTS 2:41–42 SKJV

The Best Way to Live

Many "books" of the New Testament are letters. They were written by people like Paul, Peter, and John. These letters were sent to people and churches. The letters told people how to live for Jesus. They teach us about loving God. They teach us about loving others. They teach us the best way to live.

Do not let yourselves get tired of doing good. If we do not give up, we will get what is coming to us at the right time.
GALATIANS 6:9

Remember to do good and help each other. Gifts like this please God.
HEBREWS 13:16

God's Big Plan

The last book of the Bible is called Revelation. It tells how God will make things right again one day. It says Jesus will come back to earth. He will be King of everything. His love and goodness will win forever!

"See! I am coming soon. I am bringing with Me the reward I will give to everyone for what he has done. I am the First and the Last. I am the beginning and the end. Those who wash their clothes clean are happy (who are washed by the blood of the Lamb). They will have the right to go into the city through the gates. They will have the right to eat the fruit of the tree of life. . . . I am Jesus."

REVELATION 22:12–14, 16

The New Testament shows that Jesus saves people. We all need Him! Jesus can make us part of God's family. The New Testament is full of hope. Every word is part of the best story ever told!

Rhyme It!

Sin and sadness pass away when Jesus comes to save the day.

ACTIVITY:

Old Testament Or New Testament?

How well do you know your Bible? Let's see! Think about each story below. Then choose (O) if it happened in the Old Testament. Choose (N) if it happened in the New Testament.

Remember: The Old Testament tells about creation, God's laws, prophets, and the people before Jesus. The New Testament is about Jesus' life, the early church, and how we should live today.

Let's find out what you know. Ready. . .set. . .go!

1. God created the world in six days. **O or N**

2. Jesus walked on water. **O or N**

3. Noah built an ark to save his family and the animals from a flood. **O or N**

4. Moses received the Ten Commandments. **O or N**

5. Jesus healed a blind man. **O or N**

6. Jonah was swallowed by a big fish. **O or N**

7. David fought the giant Goliath. **O or N**

8. Jesus fed 5,000 people with five loaves and two fish. **O or N**

9. Daniel was thrown into a lions' den. **O or N**

10. Zacchaeus climbed a tree to see Jesus. **O or N**

11. Saul met Jesus on the road to Damascus. **O or N**

12. The walls of Jericho fell down. **O or N**

13. Jesus turned water into wine. **O or N**

14. Elijah beat the prophets of the false god Baal. **O or N**

15. Shadrach, Meshach, and Abednego lived through the fiery furnace. **O or N**

How did you do? Turn the page to see how many you got right.

Answers

1. O	5. N	9. O	13. N
2. N	6. O	10. N	14. O
3. O	7. O	11. N	15. O
4. O	8. N	12. O	

0–5 Correct: Bible Beginner
You're off to a great start. Keep reading! Keep learning more about God's big story.

6–10 Correct: Bible Student
You're finding out about the Bible's big story. Great job!

11–15 Correct: Bible Expert
You know a lot about God's Word. Share what you know with others!

Section Four

WHAT'S THE BIBLE ABOUT?

THE BIG PICTURE: GOD'S STORY

Have you ever painted a picture? There are lots of colors. But they make one big picture.

The Bible is like a big picture. **The Bible is one story—God's story.** It tells us all about God. It tells how God works in the world. The many parts of the Bible tell one story. It's the "big picture" of God. He made everything. People turned away from Him. God made a way to bring us back to Himself through Jesus.

Here's how all the parts fit together:

In the beginning, God made the world. He made people so they could know and love Him.

Then God said, "Let Us make man like Us
and let him be head over the fish of the sea,
and over the birds of the air, and over the cattle,
and over all the earth, and over every thing
that moves on the ground."
GENESIS 1:26

But people made bad choices. Sin came into the world. The Bible shows us how bad sin is.

This is what happened: Sin came into the world by one man, Adam. Sin brought death with it. Death spread to all men because all have sinned.
ROMANS 5:12

God still loved people! He sent a Savior to fix things. That is Jesus!

See, the Lord has made it known to the end of the earth: Say to the people of Zion, "Look, the One Who saves you is coming! See, He is bringing His reward that He will give."
ISAIAH 62:11

God showed His love through Jesus. Jesus brings us close to God. That was all part of God's plan!

He gave the right and the power to become children of God to those who received Him. He gave this to those who put their trust in His name.
JOHN 1:12

Jesus will come back to earth. He will make things right again. Then He will be King forever!

At the end of the world, Christ will give His holy nation over to God the Father. Christ will have destroyed every nation and power. Christ must be King until He has destroyed all those who hate Him and work against Him. The last thing that will be destroyed is death. The Holy Writings say that God has put all things under Christ's feet except Himself. When Christ is over all things, He will put Himself under God Who put all things under Christ. And God will be over all things.

1 CORINTHIANS 15:24–28

Every book of the Bible tells a part of God's big story. Every part points to God's love for us. The Bible is a big book. It's like a big puzzle. But when we put it all together, we see God's big story. And we get to be part of it!

GOD AND PEOPLE: HIS LOVE FOR YOU

Did you know that God loves you? Did you know God's love is the biggest love of all? Way back in the beginning, God made people. He wanted to enjoy people. **God wanted people to enjoy Him.** He didn't just make people and then forget them. He wants us to talk with Him. He wants to be a great dad to us.

The Lord came to us from far away, saying, "I have loved you with a love that lasts forever. So I have helped you come to Me with loving-kindness."
JEREMIAH 31:3

See what great love the Father has for us that He would call us His children. And that is what we are. For this reason the people of the world do not know who we are because they did not know Him. Dear friends, we are God's children now. But it has not yet been shown to us what we are going to be. We know that when He comes again, we will be like Him because we will see Him as He is.
1 JOHN 3:1–2

God's love for you is huge!

It's the kind of love that never goes away. No matter what happens, **God loves you**. And God proved His love with a very special gift. He sent His Son, Jesus, to die on the cross for people's sins. Jesus was the perfect man. He was God in a human body. Jesus paid the price for every wrong thing we ever did. Do you see how much God loves you?

Now, **God wants you to love Him back**. He wants you to love other people too. That is our job. We should love God and love others. When we do, we show the world how awesome God is.

We love Him because He loved us first.
1 JOHN 4:19

"I [Jesus] give you a new Law. You are to love each other. You must love each other as I have loved you. If you love each other, all men will know you are My followers."
JOHN 13:34–35

God loves you all the time. Even when you make a mistake. Even when you choose to do wrong. God still wants you to be close to Him. If you tell Him you did wrong, **God will forgive**. He will always help you to make things right.

For I know that nothing can keep us from the love of God. Death cannot! Life cannot! Angels cannot! Leaders cannot! Any other power cannot! Hard things now or in the future cannot! The world above or the world below cannot! Any other living thing cannot keep us away from the love of God which is ours through Christ Jesus our Lord.

ROMANS 8:38–39

The Bible says *nothing* can keep you from God's love.

Can **bad days** keep you from God's love? No! When you're sad or mad, God still loves you.

Can **mess-ups** keep you from God's love? No! God always loves and wants us to do better.

Can **losing** keep you from God's love? No! Win or lose, God still loves you just the same.

Can **big changes** keep you from God's love? No! Maybe you have to move to a new place. Maybe an important person goes out of your life. God's love stays the same.

God's love isn't based on how good you are. God's love isn't based on what you do. **When you follow Jesus, God's love for you will not change.** You can always trust that God loves you. He will love you forever and ever!

HOW SIN CAME INTO THE WORLD. . . AND WHAT JESUS DID TO FIX IT

When God made the world, everything was just right. God said it was all very good. He made people to love Him. God wanted to be friends with people. But one day, something went wrong.

The first people made a bad choice. **Adam and Eve disobeyed God.** They ate some fruit that God had told them not to eat. This was the first *sin*. Now there was trouble in the world. Sin was everywhere. People started doing bad things. They hurt themselves. They hurt other people. **And they hurt God.**

Then the Lord saw that man was very sinful on the earth. Every plan and thought of the heart of man was sinful always. The Lord was sorry that He had made man on the earth. He had sorrow in His heart.

GENESIS 6:5–6

Sin is doing anything that God hates. Lying is sin. Being unkind is sin. Stealing is sin. Thinking any kind of bad thought is sin. **Sin keeps people away from God.**

It's very sad. Every person in the world sins. No one can fix this problem by themselves.

Everyone has turned away from God.
They have all done wrong.
Not one of them does what is good.
No, not even one!
ROMANS 3:12

But God didn't want people to stay in their sin. **God sent Jesus into the world to fix what sin broke.** Jesus is God's Son. He became a human being like all of us. Jesus lived a perfect life on earth. He showed us what God's love looks like.

Jesus never, ever sinned. But He died on the cross for *our* sin. That's how much Jesus loves us! **Jesus was punished for every sin people have done.**

It was sad when Jesus died. But then He came back to life! This is called the "resurrection." Jesus is God. And He is stronger than anything else, even death.

Now, we can be right with God by believing in Jesus. He made the way for people to be saved from their sin. God wants all people to "accept" Jesus. That means we believe Jesus is God's Son. We believe Jesus became a man who died for other people's sins. We believe Jesus came back to life to prove His power.

When we do these things, we are "saved."

If you say with your mouth that Jesus is Lord, and believe in your heart that God raised Him from the dead, you will be saved from the punishment of sin.

ROMANS 10:9

Jesus fixed what sin broke. Now we can be close to God forever!

Believe that Jesus is God. Believe that He died for your sin. Believe that He came back from the dead. Then you can be part of God's family. You don't have to be perfect. You just need to trust God. He will forgive you because of what Jesus did.

Our belief in Jesus makes us God's children! That is the best news ever.

You should not act like people who are owned by someone. They are always afraid. Instead, the Holy Spirit makes us His sons, and we can call to Him, "My Father."
ROMANS 8:15

HOW TO FOLLOW JESUS

We are learning the Bible! It tells us that Jesus wants you in God's family. And God's family is *forever*. If you trust Jesus, He will always be with you. Jesus helps you in everything you do in this world. Then He gives you life that lasts forever! It is a perfect life that never ends.

Jesus wants you to follow Him. What does that mean? It's as easy as A-B-C:

Admit that you've made wrong choices. Wrong choices are sin. Ask God to forgive you.

Believe that Jesus died on the cross for your sins. And believe He rose again to give you new life.

Choose to live for Jesus every day. You do this by obeying what the Bible says.

Remember!

A-B-C = Admit, Believe, Choose

Friends Forever

We all want a good friend. And Jesus will be your best friend ever. He is always with you. Jesus helps you. Jesus shows you what to do. **Jesus loves you.** He will help you through your life on earth. And then you'll live with Jesus forever in heaven.

"Do not let your heart be troubled. You have put your trust in God, put your trust in Me also. There are many rooms in My Father's house. If it were not so, I would have told you. I am going away to make a place for you. After I go and make a place for you, I will come back and take you with Me. Then you may be where I am."

JOHN 14:1–3

What Happens When You Follow Jesus?

What is the best choice you could ever make? To follow Jesus!

Great things happen when you become a Christian. Here are some of them:

You are forgiven! Jesus washes away your sins. He gives you a fresh start.

You become part of God's family. Nothing can take God's love away from you!

You can talk to God anytime. Pray about anything. God promises to listen.

You know what life is all about. God helps you live to please Him.

You can get closer to God every day. You can read your Bible. You can pray. You can worship God. He will help you to know Him better. You will see more and more how much He loves you.

You have hope. Life can be hard. But following Jesus gives hope. Why? Because you know God is always in control. You know that God has a good plan for you.

You know you'll live forever. Following Jesus isn't just for today. Being friends with Jesus starts now and never ends!

For by His loving-favor you have been saved from the punishment of sin through faith. It is not by anything you have done. It is a gift of God.
EPHESIANS 2:8

Thank God for His great Gift.
2 CORINTHIANS 9:15

ACTIVITY:

Bible Verses to Remember

The Bible is full of great verses. Many tell of God's love for you. They tell how you can live with God forever.

Try to memorize the verses below. Keep them in your heart! They'll help you remember all the good things God has done.

In the beginning God made from nothing the heavens and the earth.
GENESIS 1:1

(God started it all—He made the world and everything in it!)

We love Him because He loved us first.
1 JOHN 4:19

(God loves you because He made you. He wants you in His family forever!)

This is what happened: Sin came into the world by one man, Adam. Sin brought death with it. Death spread to all men because all have sinned.
ROMANS 5:12

(Adam and Eve disobeyed God. That was sin. Because of sin, we all need God's help. But God loves people. He sent Jesus to save us!)

This is love! It is not that we loved God but that He loved us. For God sent His Son to pay for our sins with His own blood.
1 JOHN 4:10

(This is God's rescue plan. Jesus gave His life for us. Now we can live forever with Him.)

Jesus said, "I am the Way and the Truth and the Life. No one can go to the Father except by Me."
JOHN 14:6

(Jesus is the only way to know God. Jesus is our one true hope.)

"For sure, I tell you, he who puts his trust in Me has life that lasts forever."
JOHN 6:47

(Follow Jesus. Be part of God's family. Enjoy Him *forever*!)

Memorizing Bible Verses

It's great to memorize God's Word. It takes some work. But it's worth it!

Pick a verse to learn. Write it on a piece of paper. Write it on a note card. Write it on the inside of your Bible. Use colored pens. Draw a picture with it. Do anything to make the verse stand out. Then read and re-read the verse as often as you can. Try to say it back to yourself without looking.

Keep working on it. Before long, you'll have the verse memorized. After a while, you might have a lot of verses hidden in your heart!

"Keep these words of mine in your heart and in your soul."
DEUTERONOMY 11:18

Section Five

WHAT BIBLE STORIES SHOULD EVERYONE KNOW?

CREATION: WHERE WE COME FROM (GENESIS 1)

Once upon a time, there was no world. There was only God. But then **God made the world and everything in it.** He just spoke words and there was earth. He spoke and there was sky. He spoke and there were oceans. He spoke and there were trees and animals and plants.

The best thing God made was people. He made Adam and Eve to be like Him. They could think. They could speak. They could love. God wanted them to live with Him in the brand-new world.

Things were just right. The world was full of life. There were flowers and fish and birds. But people were the most important. They could know God.

God saw all that He had made and it was very good. There was evening and there was morning, the sixth day.
GENESIS 1:31

God shows His love by what He made. And **God made *you***!

Men cannot say they do not know about God. From the beginning of the world, men could see what God is like through the things He has made. This shows His power that lasts forever. It shows that He is God.
ROMANS 1:20

Trust in the living God, who richly gives us all things to enjoy.
1 TIMOTHY 6:17 SKJV

God made all things in just six days. What a week that was!

What God made is called "creation." Here is how the week of creation went:

Day 1: God made light. Day and night were part of what He made.

Day 2: God made the sky. There was water above and water below. The whole earth was one big ocean.

Day 3: God made dry land. Then He made plants to grow on the land.

Day 4: God made the sun, the moon, and the stars. They would give light to the world.

Day 5: God made birds and fish.

Day 6: God made animals for the land. Then, at last, God made *people*. The first people's names were Adam and Eve.

Day 7: God was done with His work. So He rested.

Everything God made was good. And He made us to enjoy it with Him!

Think About It!

Which day of creation is your favorite, and why?

NOAH'S ARK: GOD'S BIG RESCUE (GENESIS 6-8)

You might know this story! It tells how God saved Noah from a huge flood. Noah and his family built a big boat called "the ark." They were saved from the water along with lots of animals.

Because of sin, the world was very bad. Most people didn't follow God at all. **But Noah loved God.** He obeyed God's Word. So God told Noah to build the ark. The flood would destroy everything outside the ark.

God looked at the earth and saw how sinful it was. For all who lived on the earth had become sinful in their ways. Then God said to Noah, "I have decided to make an end to all the people on the earth. They are the cause of very much trouble. See, I will destroy them as I destroy the earth. Make a large boat of gopher wood for yourself."

GENESIS 6:12–14

Noah built the ark for many years. Then God told him it was time. **Noah brought two of each kind of animal.** There were birds. There were lions. There were elephants. They all went into the ark with Noah. It started to rain. It rained and rained and rained! Soon, the ark was floating on top of the water. The whole earth was covered.

Many months went by. Then the flood waters went down. The ark landed on a mountain. Noah and the animals stepped outside. They began a new life on earth.

God said He would never flood the world again. He put a rainbow in the sky as a promise.

"When I bring clouds over the earth and the rain-bow is seen in the clouds, I will remember My agreement that is between Me and you and every living thing of all flesh. Never again will the water become a flood to destroy all flesh."

GENESIS 9:14–15

More About Noah's Ark

A super-sized boat: The ark was about 450 feet long. It was 75 feet wide. That means it was bigger than a football field!

A big storm: It rained for 40 days and nights. The rain was heavy. It just kept coming for more than a month. The water covered the whole earth for five months.

A bunch of animals: Noah took two of every kind of animal with him. But there were 14 of some kinds of animals. They were called "clean" animals.

Think About It!

What do you think it was like to be on a floating zoo?

A new start: Noah and his family were the only people left on earth. They got to start over. God "blessed" them. That means He gave them good things to make them happy.

A promise for us: God put a rainbow in the sky as a promise. He said He would never again flood the whole world. Today, rainbows show us that God keeps His promises. We can always trust Him.

What can we learn from Noah's story? We learn that it's important to obey God. We learn that God hates sin. We learn that God keeps His promises.

Jesus says yes to all of God's many promises. It is through Jesus that we say, "Let it be so," when we give thanks to God.
2 CORINTHIANS 1:20

DAVID AND GOLIATH: THE SHEPHERD BOY AND THE GIANT (1 SAMUEL 17)

Goliath was a scary giant. God's people were afraid of him. No one was brave enough to face this huge enemy.

But then a shepherd boy named David stood up. He heard Goliath saying mean things. "I can fight Goliath!" David said. "God will help me!" **The young man trusted God.** David was much smaller than Goliath. David had no suit of armor. But David had faith in God.

David said to the Philistine, "You come to me with a sword and spears. But I come to you in the name of the Lord of All, the God of the armies of Israel, Whom you have stood against. This day the Lord will give you into my hands. . . . Then all the earth may know that there is a God in Israel."

1 SAMUEL 17:45–46

David didn't even have a sword. But he had a sling. He had five smooth stones. Goliath was mad. He ran toward David. But David put a stone in his sling. He swung it around and around. The stone flew right between Goliath's eyes! He fell down to the ground. David won the battle. David won because he trusted God.

David said. . ."All these people gathered here may know that the Lord does not save with sword and spear. For the battle is the Lord's and He will give you into our hands."

1 SAMUEL 17:45, 47

David had faith. He showed that *God* is stronger than anyone else.

More About David and Goliath

Goliath was more than nine feet tall. That's almost as high as a basketball hoop!

David didn't wear armor. Soldiers wore metal armor to keep themselves safe. King Saul tried to give his armor to David. It was too big and heavy. David just trusted God.

David used a slingshot. He didn't carry a sword and shield. David used a sling and five smooth stones he picked up from a stream.

David only needed one stone. He had five stones with him. But the first stone hit Goliath right in the head. The stone made the giant fall down.

The strongest man lost the fight. David was young and small. But he trusted God to help him. Faith in God is the most important thing.

David would later become a king. The boy who beat a giant would later be Israel's greatest ruler.

David won the battle because the battle belonged to God. David's size didn't matter. David's strength wasn't important. **David's God was the reason he won!** God will win every battle He fights.

"The Lord says to you, 'Do not be afraid or troubled because of these many men. For the battle is not yours but God's.'"
2 CHRONICLES 20:15

THE FIRST CHRISTMAS: A KING IS BORN

A long time ago, God made a big promise. He would send a Savior to the world! **The Savior was Jesus.** Here is the story of His birth.

A girl named Mary was planning to get married. Her husband would be Joseph. Mary loved Joseph. And Mary loved God. God loved Mary too, and gave her a very important job. **God told Mary that she would have a baby.** But she wouldn't have the baby with Joseph. Mary's baby would be the Son of God!

It was almost time for the baby to be born. Mary and Joseph had to go to a little town called Bethlehem. There was no place to stay. So they slept in a place where animals were kept. That night, Mary had her baby! Jesus would grow up to save the world.

The angel said to them, "Do not be afraid. See! I bring you good news of great joy which is for all people. Today, One Who saves from the punishment of sin has been born in the city of David. He is Christ the Lord."

LUKE 2:10–11

More About the Birth of Jesus

Jesus is God's Son. Jesus wasn't a regular baby. He was God's Son! Jesus came to earth to save people. His birth was part of God's big plan to rescue people from sin.

God's promise came true. Prophets wrote about Jesus long before He was born. They said a Savior would come. And Jesus did!

For to us a Child will be born. To us a Son will be given. And the rule of the nations will be on His shoulders. His name will be called Wonderful, Teacher, Powerful God, Father Who Lives Forever, Prince of Peace. There will be no end to His rule and His peace, upon the throne of David and over his nation.He will build it to last and keep it strong with what is right and fair and good from that time and forever. The work of the Lord of All will do this.

ISAIAH 9:6–7

Jesus was poor. Jesus is the King of all kings. But He wasn't born in a palace. Jesus was born where animals are kept. His first bed was a feeding box.

God wanted normal people in His story. Mary was a normal girl. Working men like shepherds were first told about Jesus' birth.

Jesus was born for everyone. Jesus came to earth for *all* of us. You don't have to be rich. You don't have to be important. Jesus wants to save you!

Then Peter said, "I can see, for sure, that God does not respect one person more than another. He is pleased with any man in any nation who honors Him and does what is right."
ACTS 10:34–35

Think About It!

Are you a kid who honors God and does what is right?

THE RESURRECTION: JESUS IS ALIVE!

Jesus died on a cross. His friends were very sad. They put His body in a tomb. Then they rolled a big stone in front of the door. Many people had put their hope in Jesus. But now He was dead.

But Jesus didn't stay dead!

On the third day, Jesus' friends went to His tomb. They saw that the stone was rolled away. The tomb was empty!

Then a glowing angel showed up. He told Jesus' friends,

"He is not here!
He has risen from the dead
as He said He would."
MATTHEW 28:6

Jesus was alive again! He had said He would come back to life. Jesus' friends were so glad! **He told them to share the good news.**

Jesus is stronger than death. That means *we* can live forever with Him. On the cross, Jesus took the punishment for sin. Then He made a way for us to live forever with God.

Jesus said, "I am the Way and the Truth and the Life. No one can go to the Father except by Me."
JOHN 14:6

Now that we have been made right with God by putting our trust in Him, we have peace with Him. It is because of what our Lord Jesus Christ did for us. By putting our trust in God, He has given us His loving-favor and has received us. We are happy for the hope we have of sharing the shining-greatness of God.
ROMANS 5:1–2

Why It's Important That Jesus Is Alive

Jesus came back to life from the dead. That changed everything! We remember this on Easter Sunday. But we can celebrate all the time! We know that Jesus is alive. This puts hope and joy in our lives.

Jesus proved that He is the strongest. Not even death can stop Him! The Bible says this is a very important truth.

If the dead are not raised, then not even Christ was raised from the dead. If Christ was not raised from the dead, your faith is worth nothing and you are still living in your sins. Then the Christians who have already died are lost in sin. If we have hope in Christ in this life only, we are more sad than anyone else. But it is true! Christ has been raised from the dead! He was the first One to be raised from the dead and all those who are in graves will follow.

1 CORINTHIANS 15:16–20

Jesus is alive! And here is why that means so much to us:

Nothing can stop Jesus. Not even death could beat Jesus. He came back to life! Jesus has power over all things.

Jesus proved He is God's Son. By coming back to life, Jesus proved that He really is God's Son. We can trust that Jesus is able to save us.

We can have eternal life with God. Jesus is alive forever. And He can give *us* eternal life with Him. To live forever with Him, we just have to believe in Jesus.

If you say with your mouth that Jesus is Lord, and believe in your heart that God raised Him from the dead, you will be saved from the punishment of sin.
ROMANS 10:9

God keeps His promises. Jesus said He would come back to life. Then He did! This proves that God keeps His promises. We can trust Him.

Jesus is our hope. We know that Jesus is alive. So we can also know that God has power to make things right. Even when things look bad, God can make them good. Jesus changed the whole world when He came back to life! He showed that death is not the end. He showed that we can have new life through Him. Jesus is alive! And we have the hope of living forever like He does.

Nothing is too hard for Jesus. Nothing is too hard for God!

When His followers heard this, they could not understand it. They said, "Then who can be saved from the punishment of sin?" Jesus looked at them and said, "This cannot be done by men. But with God all things can be done."

MATTHEW 19:25–26

Section Six

HOW DO I READ MY BIBLE?

START A BIBLE ADVENTURE

Your Bible is like a treasure chest. God's Word is full of great things. There are exciting stories. There are promises from God. **You can read the Bible yourself!** Here are some ideas for you.

Choose a Bible you can understand. Ask a trusted grownup to help you find a good Bible. Maybe your mom or dad will know one. Maybe your pastor or teacher will. There are Bibles that use clear, simple words for kids.

Pray before you read. Ask God to help you understand what you see. God wrote the Bible! So He can speak to your heart through His Word.

If you do not have wisdom, ask God for it. He is always ready to give it to you and will never say you are wrong for asking. You must have faith as you ask Him. You must not doubt. Anyone who doubts is like a wave which is pushed around by the sea.

JAMES 1:5–6

Start reading in the New Testament. Start with the Gospels. The books of Matthew, Mark, Luke, and John are a great place to begin. They tell the story of Jesus.

Read a little each day. Don't try to read too much. Start with a small section. Read a few verses or one chapter. Take your time. Bible reading isn't a race! Read as much as you can really understand.

Ask questions. Talk to adults you trust. Ask your parents or teachers or pastor. They can help to explain the hard parts of the Bible.

He who is taught God's Word should share the good things he has with his teacher.
GALATIANS 6:6

More Advice for New Bible Readers

Here are some ideas to help you *keep* reading your Bible:

Read a little each day. Plan a time to spend with God's Word. The more you read, the more you'll grow.

Keep going. You might be confused at times. But pray and keep reading. God will help you understand when the time is right.

Make notes or draw pictures. Use your eyes and your *hands* when you read. That might help you to remember important things.

"Each of you take up a stone on his shoulder, according to the number of the tribes of the children of Israel, that this may be a sign among you when your children ask their fathers in the future, saying, 'What do you mean by these stones?' Then you shall answer them that the waters of the Jordan were cut off before the ark of the covenant of the LORD. When it crossed over the Jordan, the waters of the Jordan were cut off. And these stones shall be a memorial to the children of Israel forever."

JOSHUA 4:5–7 SKJV

It's okay if you miss a day. Don't feel bad if you miss a day. Just start again where you left off. Ask God to help you keep going. He's very patient with us.

Share what you learn. You're doing something exciting! Tell others what you find. Don't be afraid to share God's Word.

Always pray. We said this before. But it's so important that we'll say it again. The Bible is not just a book. It's God's way of talking to you. Talk to Him about what you read.

The person who is not a Christian does not understand these words from the Holy Spirit. He thinks they are foolish. He cannot understand them because he does not have the Holy Spirit to help him understand.

1 CORINTHIANS 2:14

THINK ABOUT WHAT YOU READ

It's great to read your Bible. But be sure to *think* about what you read. Some important questions will help. Ask yourself,

What is this part of the Bible all about?

Sometimes a verse or story is hard to understand. Ask yourself, "What is the biggest thing God is saying here?"

What does this part of the Bible tell me about God?

Look for clues about who God is. Look for what He's like. You can learn something about God on every page of your Bible.

The Lord is good to all. And His loving-kindness is over all His works.
PSALM 145:9

What does this part of the Bible teach about people?

Think about how the people in the story behave. What can you learn from their choices?

What does this part of the Bible mean to my life?

God's Word isn't just a story. The Bible helps us love God. The Bible helps us live better. Think how you can use what you read to make better choices.

Obey the Word of God. If you hear only and do not act, you are only fooling yourself. Anyone who hears the Word of God and does not obey is like a man looking at his face in a mirror. After he sees himself and goes away, he forgets what he looks like.

JAMES 1:22–24

Let's Practice: Dig into Your Bible

The Bible can change your life! Its tells us about God's love. It tells us how we should behave. It is full of great stories. One story is about a man named Zacchaeus. People didn't like Zacchaeus. He collected taxes. That means he took money from people. But then Zacchaeus met Jesus. His life changed for good.

Remember the questions we just learned? Let's use them to dig into the story of Zacchaeus. Let's see what God wants us to learn!

If you have your Bible, look up Luke 19. You can also find Luke 19 online, if that's okay with your parents.

What is this part of the Bible all about?

Jesus came to find lost people. He wants to save people! It doesn't matter who they are or what they've done.

What does this part of the Bible tell me about God?

God loves and forgives. That is why Jesus went right to Zacchaeus. God sees our hearts and knows when we want to change. God's kindness helps us live in a way that pleases Him.

What does this part of the Bible teach about people?

People can change. Zacchaeus was selfish at first. Zacchaeus was not honest. But when he met Jesus, he wanted to be different. Jesus will love and forgive anyone!

What does this part of the Bible mean to my life?

We should be like Zacchaeus. We should want to change when we have done wrong. We can also be kind and giving. That's how Zacchaeus was after he met Jesus.

WHAT IF I DON'T UNDERSTAND A VERSE?

Don't worry. Sometimes you won't understand. It happens to everyone! **The Bible is full of big ideas.** Some parts of the Bible take time to "get."

Here's what to do when you're stuck:

Pray and ask God for help. God *wants* you to understand His Word. So ask Him to teach you.

Ask for help from a trusted adult. A parent, a teacher, or a pastor might help. They can explain verses you don't understand.

Look for the "big picture." One verse might be confusing. So think about what the whole story is about.

Keep at it. You might not understand everything right now. But keep reading! You'll learn a little more every day.

Remember, Bible reading is not a race. The first time you read a verse, you might not understand. That's all right! **Read, pray, and ask questions.** You'll start to understand. Know that God is always with you. He will help you to learn more about Him every day.

Show me Your ways, O Lord. Teach me Your paths. Lead me in Your truth and teach me. For You are the God Who saves me. I wait for You all day long.
PSALM 25:4–5

Teach me Your way, O Lord. I will walk in Your truth. May my heart fear Your name.
PSALM 86:11

Be a Bible Detective!

Do you know what a detective is? That is a person who solves a mystery. Sometimes, the Bible is confusing. It can feel like a mystery that needs to be solved.

Here is how to be a Bible detective:

Look for clues. When you read one verse, look at the other verses around it. They might make things clear for you.

Ask the experts. Who in your life knows the Bible well? Maybe your mom or dad reads the Bible a lot. Maybe an older brother or sister knows a lot. Maybe a teacher or pastor can help.

Use Bible tools. Books like this one can help! And there are special Bibles just for kids. If your parents say it's okay, look up Bible information online.

Don't give up! Keep reading. Keep praying. Keep thinking. It may take some time. But remember that God *wants* you to know His Word. Trust Him to help you in His good time.

Do not let yourselves get tired
of doing good. If we do not give up,
we will get what is coming to
us at the right time.
GALATIANS 6:9

A Prayer for Learning the Bible!

Lord God, I want to know Your Word better. Since You wrote it, will You please help me understand it? I want to know what You've said. I want to live my life in obedience. Thank You!

WHAT SHOULD I READ?

There are lots of great stories in the Bible! Do you like to read about armies and battles? Do you like love stories? Do you like to know how the world works? You'll find all of these things in the Bible.

On the next few pages are ideas for parts of the Bible to read. Some are stories about people. Some are verses about important ideas. Look them up in your own Bible. Or if your parents say it's okay, look them up online.

Everything that was written
in the Holy Writings long ago
was written to teach us.
ROMANS 15:4

IMPORTANT PEOPLE: Abraham (read Genesis 12:1–8)

Abraham was a man of faith. He believed what God told him. God chose Abraham for a special job. He would start a nation of God's people called Israel. But Abraham was old. He didn't have any kids. So God helped Abraham's wife to have a baby. His name was Isaac. It was a miracle!

The Holy Writings say,
"Abraham put his trust in God
and that made him right with God."
ROMANS 4:3

IMPORTANT PEOPLE: Jacob (read Genesis 35:9–14)

Jacob was the grandson of Abraham. God gave Jacob the same promise He gave to Abraham. God said Jacob's family would be large. It would be a whole nation. They would be God's special people. One time, Jacob wrestled with God. **God changed Jacob's name to Israel.**

And the man said, "Your name
will no longer be Jacob, but Israel.
For you have fought with God
and with men, and have won."
GENESIS 32:28

IMPORTANT PEOPLE: Deborah (read Judges 4:1–10)

Deborah was a strong woman. She was the leader of Israel. She also led soldiers in war. **Deborah was called a "judge."** Judges were leaders in Israel before there was a king.

Now Lappidoth's wife Deborah,
a woman who spoke for God,
was judging Israel at that time.
JUDGES 4:4

IMPORTANT PEOPLE: Ruth (read Ruth 1:1–18)

Ruth was a kind woman. She loved her mother-in-law Naomi. Then both of their husbands died. Ruth didn't want to leave Naomi. She helped Naomi to find food to eat. Then Ruth met a kind man named Boaz. He married Ruth and she had a baby. Many years later, Jesus was born into Ruth's family line!

But Ruth said, "Do not beg me to leave you or turn away from following you. I will go where you go. I will live where you live. Your people will be my people. And your God will be my God."
RUTH 1:16

IMPORTANT PEOPLE: Solomon (read 1 Kings 3:5–14)

Solomon was a wise king. He was the son of David. **God gave Solomon more wisdom than any other man.** God also made Solomon rich. He built a temple for God. But later, Solomon made big mistakes. He turned away from God. His country split in two. At the end of his life, Solomon came back to God.

The last word, after all has been heard, is:
Honor God and obey His Laws.
This is all that every person must do.
ECCLESIASTES 12:13

IMPORTANT PEOPLE: Josiah (read 2 Kings 23:1–3)

Josiah became king at age eight! He loved God and did what was right. First, he taught his people to obey God's laws. Then he built God's temple again. It had been destroyed in a battle. Josiah made the people stop worshipping false gods.

Josiah did what is right in the eyes of the Lord.
He walked in all the way of his father David.
He did not turn aside to the right or to the left.
2 KINGS 22:2

IMPORTANT PEOPLE: Daniel (read Daniel 6:1–22)

Daniel was a prophet. He told people what God showed him. Daniel could even say what dreams meant! Some bad people got Daniel in trouble. They tricked the king who put Daniel into a lions' den. But God sent an angel to help Daniel. It shut the lions' mouths. Daniel wasn't hurt at all. He was saved because he trusted God.

Daniel showed that he could do better work than the other leaders and captains because a special spirit was in him. So the king planned to give him power over the whole nation.

DANIEL 6:3

IMPORTANT PEOPLE: Shadrach, Meshach, and Abednego (read Daniel 3:8–27)

These three men were friends of Daniel. They would not worship a false god. So the evil king threw them into a fiery furnace. But **God saved Shadrach, Meshach, and Abednego**. They were not burned at all.

"Praise be to the God of Shadrach, Meshach, and Abed-nego. He has sent His angel and saved His servants who put their trust in Him. They changed the king's word and were ready to give up their lives instead of serving or worshiping any god except their own God."

DANIEL 3:28

IMPORTANT PEOPLE: Esther (read Esther 4:4–17)

Esther was Jewish. She was one of God's special people. But Esther lived in a faraway country. The king wanted a new queen. Esther was very pretty. She was chosen to marry the king! Then she learned someone wanted to kill all the Jews. **Esther was very brave.** She stood up for her people. God saved them all!

"If you keep quiet at this time, help will come to the Jews from another place. But you and your father's house will be destroyed. Who knows if you have not become queen for such a time as this?"
ESTHER 4:14

IMPORTANT PEOPLE: Jesus (read John 3:1–17)

Jesus is the Son of God. **Jesus is the Savior of the world.** Jesus made the whole world. Then He came to His world to live as a man. Jesus died on the cross to pay the price for sin. Now He saves people from sin every day. Without Jesus, no one would ever go to heaven.

"There is no way to be saved from the punishment of sin through anyone else. For there is no other name under heaven given to men by which we can be saved."
ACTS 4:12

IMPORTANT PEOPLE: Peter (read Acts 3:1–10)

Peter was one of Jesus' closest friends. Peter was also called Simon. Before he followed Jesus, Peter was a fisherman. Peter could be bold. He talked a lot. But sometimes Peter was afraid of other people. When Jesus was arrested, Peter said he didn't even know Him. But Jesus forgave Peter. And **Peter became an important leader in the new church**.

Peter said to them, "Be sorry for your sins and turn from them and be baptized in the name of Jesus Christ, and your sins will be forgiven. You will receive the gift of the Holy Spirit."
ACTS 2:38

IMPORTANT PEOPLE: Paul (read Acts 9:1–19)

Paul was first called Saul. He hated Jesus. He hated people who followed Jesus. Saul tried to stop the good news about Jesus. But then Jesus stopped Saul! Saul was on a road when a bright light shined on him. Jesus spoke to Saul. Saul listened! He started to follow Jesus. Before long, Saul was called Paul. He went from city to city telling people about Jesus. **Paul was a great missionary.** Paul also wrote many books of the Bible.

I have worked hard and have been tired and have had pain. I have gone many times without sleep. I have been hungry and thirsty. I have gone without food and clothes. I have been out in the cold. More than all these things that have happened to my body, the care of all the churches is heavy on me.
2 CORINTHIANS 11:27–28

BIG IDEAS: Temptation (read James 1:13–25)

When you are "tempted," you feel like doing what you know is wrong. **Everyone is tempted at some time.** Even Jesus! (Read how Satan tempted Jesus in Matthew 4:1–11.) The Lord's Prayer teaches us to ask God for help. Jesus said we should pray that God would keep us away from temptation. The Bible says God will help us when we are tempted.

You have never been tempted to sin in any different way than other people. God is faithful. He will not allow you to be tempted more than you can take. But when you are tempted, He will make a way for you to keep from falling into sin.

1 CORINTHIANS 10:13

BIG IDEAS: Sin (read 1 John 1:5–10)

Sin is the bad things people do. **Sin is disobeying God.** The first people to sin were Adam and Eve. From then on, everyone has sinned. As hard as we try, we can never be perfect like God. The good news is that God forgives. We must tell Him what we did wrong and be truly sorry. Jesus died to pay for our sins. God forgives us because Jesus took the punishment.

You get what is coming to you when you sin. It is death! But God's free gift is life that lasts forever. It is given to us by our Lord Jesus Christ.

ROMANS 6:23

BIG IDEAS: Salvation (read 1 Timothy 1:6–11)

"Salvation" is a work that God does. He saves people by taking them out of their sin. **To be saved, you need to believe in Jesus.** You admit that you are a sinner. You agree that Jesus is the only way to God. You ask Him to forgive you and change your life. Would you like to be saved right now? Pray this prayer: "Dear Jesus, I am sorry for the bad things I have done. I believe that You died on the cross for me. Please take away my sins and save me. Thank You." Now you have been saved!

As he took them outside, he said, "Sirs, what must I do to be saved?" They said, "Put your trust in the Lord Jesus Christ and you and your family will be saved from the punishment of sin."

ACTS 16:30–31

BIG IDEAS: Holiness (read 1 Peter 1:13–19)

To be "holy" is to be set apart for God. God is holy. And God wants His people to be holy too. Jesus is called the Holy One of God. Nobody can be perfect like He is. But He will save you when you ask. And then you should try your best to be like Him.

Even before the world was made, God chose us for Himself because of His love. He planned that we should be holy and without blame as He sees us.

EPHESIANS 1:4

BIG IDEAS: Worship (read John 4:19–24)

To "worship" is to think and say good things about God. You can worship God at church. And you can worship God anywhere you go! You can worship God by yourself or with others. **Your whole life should be about worshipping God.** Have you worshipped God today? Take some time to tell Him how great He is.

Christian brothers, I ask you from my heart to give your bodies to God because of His loving-kindness to us. Let your bodies be a living and holy gift given to God. He is pleased with this kind of gift. This is the true worship that you should give Him.

ROMANS 12:1

BIG IDEAS: Fruit (read Galatians 5:22–26)

Sometimes the Bible talks about fruit like grapes or apples. But "fruit" has a more important meaning. The "fruit of the Spirit" is **the good stuff God grows in our lives** as we follow Jesus. Love is a fruit of the Spirit. So is peace. So is joy. Can you think of anything sweeter?

"A good tree cannot have bad fruit.
A bad tree cannot have good fruit.
For every tree is known by its own fruit.
Men do not gather figs from thorns.
They do not gather grapes from thistles."

LUKE 6:43–44

BIG IDEAS: Church (read Ephesians 1:15–23)

In the Bible, the "church" is all of God's people. When you think of the word *church*, you might think of a building. But **the church is all the people who belong to Jesus**. God's people get together in a church building to worship Him. Jesus is the head of the church. The church helps Christians grow in their faith.

God is able to do much more than we ask or think through His power working in us. May we see His shining-greatness in the church. May all people in all time honor Christ Jesus. Let it be so.
EPHESIANS 3:20–21

BIG IDEAS: Heaven (read John 14:1–7)

Heaven is God's home. Jesus said He is making a place for His followers in heaven. Jesus said He would come again and take us to be with Him forever. Heaven is a beautiful, happy place. It will be our great reward.

We will receive the great things that we have been promised. They are being kept safe in heaven for us. They are pure and will not pass away. They will never be lost.
1 PETER 1:4

MORE GREAT READING FOR KIDS

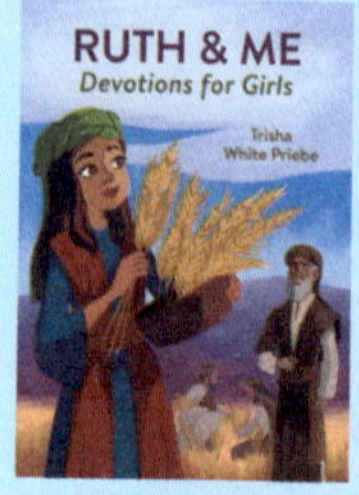

979-8-89151-123-1

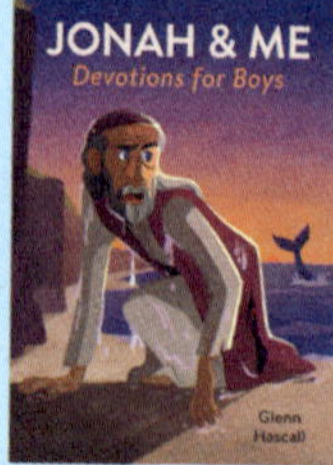

979-8-89151-122-4

979-1-63609-624-7

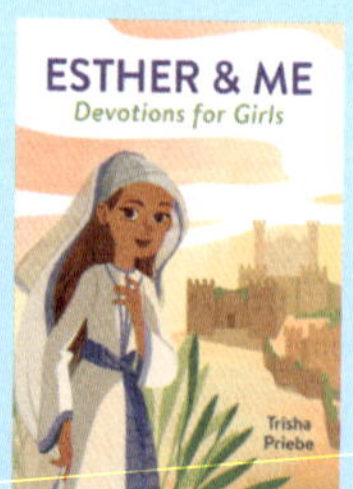

979-1-63609-620-9

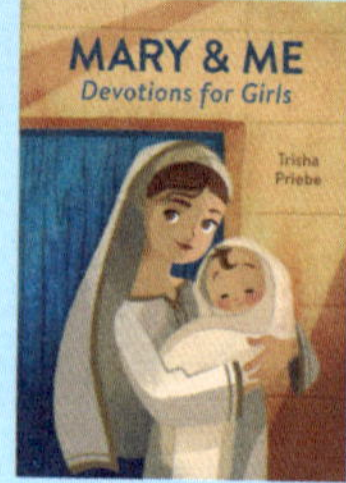

979-1-63609-857-9

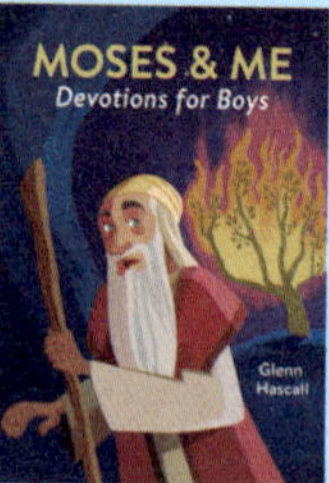

979-1-63609-852-4

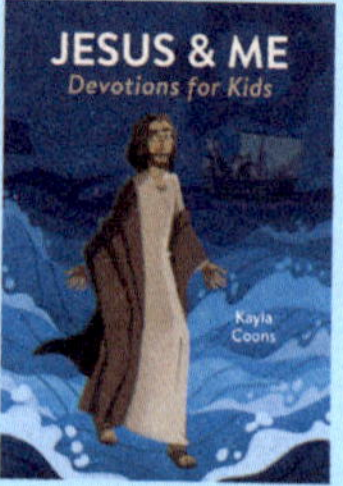

979-8-89151-343-3

You can learn a lot from the stories of Ruth, Jonah, David, Esther, Mary, Moses, and Jesus—and these devotionals for 5-to-8-year-olds make the learning fun! You'll see how each character's life and yours are often alike—and be encouraged to follow the good examples they set.

Paperback / 96 pages each